GOLD
RUSH!

Other Books by James Klein

———————————

Where to Find Gold in Southern California

Where to Find Gold in the Desert

Where to Find Gold in the Mother Lode

Where to Find Gold and Gems in Nevada

Drywashing for Gold

How to Find Gold

GOLD RUSH!

THE YOUNG PROSPECTOR'S GUIDE TO STRIKING IT RICH

Written by James Klein

Illustrated by Michael Rohani

Tricycle Press
Berkeley, California

Tricycle Press
P.O. Box 7123
Berkeley, California 94707

Book packaged by Beyond Words Publishing, Inc.
Interior design and composition by Rohani Design
Cover design by Gary Bernal
Book edited by Trevor Jacobson

Library of Congress Cataloging-in-Publication Data
Klein, James, 1932-
    Gold Rush! : the young prospector's guide to striking it rich / written by James Klein ; illustrated by Michael Rohani.
        p. cm.
        Summary: Discusses the creation, history, and location of gold, describes tools used by prospectors, and provides instructions on how to find and pan for gold.
        ISBN 1-883672-64-3
        1. Gold mines and mining—United States—Juvenile literature. 2. Prospecting—United States—Juvenile literature. 3. Gold—Juvenile literature. 4. California—Gold discoveries—History—Juvenile literature. [1. Gold mines and mining. 2. Prospecting. 3. Gold.] I. Rohani, Michael, ill. II. Title.
    TN423.A5K53 1998
    622'.3422—DC21   97-40446
                                                                                  CIP
                                                                                  AC

First Tricycle Press Printing, 1998
Printed in Canada

1 2 3 4 5 6 — 02 01 00 99 98

For my seven kids, who have always made it fun going out looking for the bright yellow stuff ... GOLD!

—James

CONTENTS

COULD YOU
STRIKE IT RICH?

It was 1851, Mariposa County, California. The gold rush was in full swing and the Sherlock Creek camp was like many others in the area. The men spent their days furiously digging for gold, while the young boys who lived in the camp went into the woods to try to strike it rich themselves.

One hot summer day, a young Mexican boy (his name was never recorded in history books) wandered into the woods with his dog. As he was walking he noticed something shining on the rocky ground. He brought the rock back to camp to show the others.

The miners quickly realized the rock was quartz and the shiny stuff was gold! They asked him to go back and mark the spot where he'd found it. The next day, the boy set out again.

He did find the spot again and sure enough he found another shiny rock. He put it in his pocket and began searching for more. A few feet away he found another one, and a few feet farther, another. He followed the trail of shiny rocks up the side of a mountain until he came to a hole in the ground.

He couldn't believe his eyes. The hole was totally filled with the shiny rocks and pure gold nuggets! The boy was so excited by his discovery that he didn't hear his dog growling, and when he finally looked up and saw a huge grizzly bear strolling his way, it was almost too late. He was just able to crawl away before the bear saw him.

He and his dog ran all the way back to camp and he showed the miners all the quartz and gold he had collected. He also told them about the amazing riches he'd seen.

About 30 men went back to the mountainside, but none of them ever found the "Cavern of Gold." They did find lots of other gold in the area though, and the Diltz Mine was formed to take the riches from the ground. This mine has since produced several million dollars worth of gold, at today's prices. One nugget they found there weighed 832 ounces (24 kilograms)!

To this day no one has found the lost "Cavern of Gold." Who knows? Maybe you will be the lucky prospector to prove that the young boy was right and dig up his lost fortune! Good luck!

A prospector with his burro. (Courtesy of Title Insurance and Trust Company)

NUGGETS OF WISDOM

FUN FACTS ABOUT GOLD

★ Gold is so heavy that a solid gold golf ball would weigh more than a brick.

★ Gold can be hammered so thin that a cup of it could be flattened over an entire football field.

★ All the gold that has so far been discovered in the world could fit inside your school gym.

★ Gold is so strong that a gold hammer could break down an iron door.

★ Gold is so rare and hard to find that in ancient times only kings, queens and other rulers had enough workers to collect it. Gold became a symbol of wealth and power . . . and still is!

★ Gold is so valuable that the ancient Egyptians actually believed it was sacred and gave magic power to its owner. They buried their rulers with many gold objects so the gold's power and magic would help them in the afterlife.

★ Gold is so durable that a piece of gold jewelry will have the same beautiful shine for thousands of years. It will not rust or tarnish, even if it is buried in the ground or under water.

★ Gold is so lasting that it can be used over and over again by melting it down and making it into new objects. Just think, the gold in your mother's wedding ring or your dad's watch could have come from the treasure in a Pharaoh's tomb!

★ Experts believe that only 10% of the gold in California has been discovered. That means there is still plenty of gold for *you* to find!

WHAT IS GOLD?

Gold is a mineral found in **veins** and **placer deposits**. A gold vein is formed when **molten rock** (lava), from deep inside the earth, eats its way to the surface. As this molten rock cools, large amounts of liquids and gases are given off. Some of these liquids and gases soak into the nearest rock, but most follow cracks, sometimes for miles, and deposit mineral matter along these cracks, forming a vein. Most gold veins are found in quartz, but they can occur in other kinds of rock too.

When veins reach the earth's surface they may be broken down by wind, cold, heat or by water running over the vein and carrying off the material. Wherever

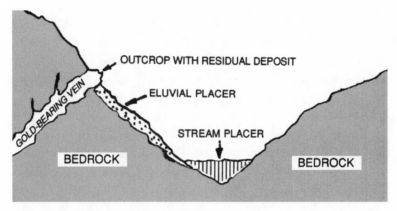

Gold vein and placer deposits. Gold deposits are moved downhill by water and erosion which separates the gold from its origin.

the water slows down or gets blocked, the heavier gold gets left behind. The area where the gold collects is called a placer deposit.

OUNCES, POUNDS OR KARATS?

Gold is always measured in ounces instead of pounds (there are 16 ounces in a pound). This is because gold is so rare that it is usually found in very small amounts.

The amount of gold within an object is measured in karats. If you have a 24 karat ring, it is pure gold.

24 karat = 100% pure gold

18 karat = 75% gold

14 karat = 58% gold

12 karat = 50% gold

10 karat = 42% gold

6 karat = 25% gold

THE VALUE OF GOLD

The value of gold changes every day. When a dollar amount of a gold discovery is mentioned in this book, it is the value of the gold when it was found. If a miner in 1850 found a nugget worth $10 dollars, nowadays that same gold nugget would be worth about $300 dollars!

WHERE DOES ALL THE GOLD GO?

34% is used to make jewelry
34% people buy for investments
9% is used to make electronics
5% is used in people's teeth
5% is used to make industrial machines
4% is used to make coins
3% is owned privately
1% is used to make medals
5% other

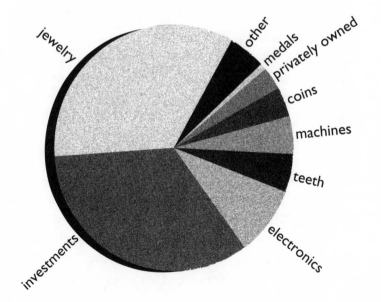

CHAPTER

3

CAVEMEN MINERS AND THE HISTORY OF GOLD FEVER

THE CRO-MAGNONS AND EGYPTIANS

Humans have always been fascinated by gold. The earliest recorded mining was in Egypt, but even the cavemen were aware of gold's special qualities. Handmade objects of gold have been found in the caves of Europe, dating back 30,000 years ago to Cro-Magnon man.

Around 2575 B.C., the Egyptians began mining millions of ounces of gold from placer deposits along the Nile River. To mine so much gold they needed a lot of help, so if you were caught committing a crime or were captured in battle there was a pretty good chance you would end up working in the gold mines as a slave.

Whether you were a man or a woman, young or old, there was work to do. Young boys picked up the rocks broken off by the miners and took them to be crushed by the women and older men. It was miserable work.

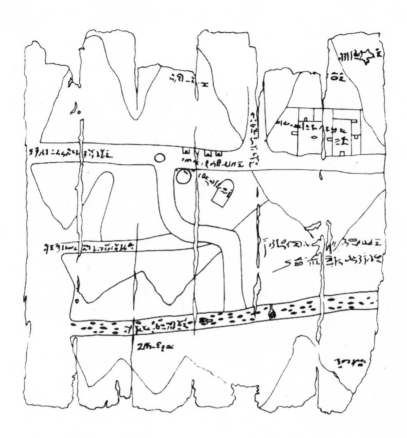

Ancient Egyptian map showing location of a gold mine.

THE ROMANS

A few thousand years later, the Romans were the first to discover new ways to mine more gold with less effort. They developed a method where they heated the rock, then threw cold water on it, which caused it to crack and shatter. Then they could pick the gold pieces out of the rock. This was much easier than crushing the rock by hand, as the Egyptians and other early miners did.

THE AMERICAS

By the 1500s, rulers in Europe began looking for new sources of gold to increase their wealth. It just so happened that in Central and South America, Indians had been mining gold for thousands of years. When Spanish explorers discovered all the gold the Indians had collected, Spain became the richest nation in the world. In just 50 years (1550–1600) Spain stole over 32 million ounces (907,000 kilograms) of gold from the Indians!

By the 1700s, Spanish missionaries had established many settlements along the California coast. The Indians, who knew how much Spaniards and other Europeans liked gold, brought the priests gold nuggets to trade for goods. When the missionaries realized there was gold close by, they started several mines and forced the Indians to mine the gold for them.

THE FIRST GOLD RUSHES IN THE UNITED STATES

On the other side of the continent in New England, the earliest settlers were also mining for gold. As the population of the United States grew and communication became easier, discoveries of gold often caused people to drop everything and "rush" to the area where gold was discovered.

One of the first gold rushes in the newly formed United States was in Georgia. A young boy found a gold nugget in a stream bed and brought it home to show his father. When the father saw the nugget, he had the boy take him to the spot where he found it. They found more gold and began mining. Word soon spread and others rushed to the area to try to strike it

The Oak of the Golden Dream. Site of the first discovery of gold in California. (Courtesy of James Klein)

rich. The rush was not very large, but some gold is still being found today in Georgia.

In March, 1842, a ranch hand named Francisco Lopez y Arballo was eating his lunch under a large oak tree in Placerita Canyon near Newhall, California. He used his knife to dig up a wild onion to eat, and found gold nuggets attached to the onion's roots! This was the beginning of the first recorded gold rush in California history. It was a very small rush, but turned out to be just the tip of the gold iceberg. Six years later a larger gold discovery in California would affect the entire world.

C H A P T E R

THE CALIFORNIA
GOLD RUSH

EUREKA!

Before the discovery of gold, California was a land of large ranches, small towns and few people. On January 24th, 1848, a small nugget of gold was found in the American River near an area which is now the town of Coloma, California. That one little nugget changed everything!

It all started when Johann August Sutter built a fort in the area, and he needed more lumber. He hired James W. Marshall, a carpenter at the fort, to build and operate a sawmill in the nearby mountains. While building this mill, Marshall made the great discovery. Here is Marshall's story in his own words.

"In May, 1847, with my rifle, blanket and a few crackers to eat with the venison (for the deer then were plentiful), I ascended the American River to find a good site for a sawmill, where we could have plenty

of timber, and where they would be able to ascend and descend the river hills. I had been out several days and reached this place, which looked like the exact spot we were hunting."[1]

Marshall and his men, with the help of local Native American tribes such as the Yalesumni, Miwok and Nisenan, built the sawmill right next to the American River. In order to turn the giant saws that cut the trees into boards (they didn't have any electricity then!), they used the power of the flowing water.

James Marshall

They funneled the river water into a small wooden channel, called a **mill race**. The water rushed into the mill race, through the sawmill, and then back out into the regular river channel. As you can imagine, the mill race collected all sorts of junk (leaves, sticks, rocks, etc.) from the river. Luckily for Marshall, he made sure to clean it out *himself* every day.

"One morning in January, it was a clear cold morning, I shall never forget that morning, as I was taking my usual walk along the mill race after turning off the water, my eye was caught with the glimpse of something shining in the bottom of the ditch. There was about a foot of water running then. I reached my hand down and picked it up, it made my heart thump, for I was certain it was gold. The piece was about the size and the shape of a pea.

Then I saw another piece in the water. After taking it out I sat down . . . to think right hard.

Sutter's Mill (Courtesy of M. Broman)

I thought it was gold and yet it did not seem to be of the right color. Putting one of the pieces on a hard river stone, I took another and commenced hammering it. It was soft and didn't break, therefore it must be gold." [2]

Marshall took the gold he and his men had collected to Mr. Sutter to find out its value. Here's what Sutter remembers about Marshall's visit:

"He was soaked to the skin and dripping water. He told me he had something of the utmost importance to tell me, that he wanted to speak to me in private, and begged me to take him to some isolated place where no one could overhear us. We went up to the next floor, and although there was no one in the house except the

bookkeeper, he insisted so strongly that we locked our-selves in the room and bolted the door."[3]

They tested the nuggets and found that Marshall was right: they were pure gold. Sutter's and Marshall's lives would never be the same and the discovery would change the world.

THE RUSH BEGINS

At first they tried to keep it a secret, fearing the workers would leave their jobs to dig the gold and not finish the mill. Sutter was able to convince the men to continue working on the mill and mine the gold only on Sundays.

The closest place for the workers to spend the gold they found was a store in Sutterville, a few miles below Sutter's Fort. It was run by a man named Sam Brannan. It wasn't long before Brannan got curious about where the gold was coming from. When he learned the

Miners with a mule train. (Courtesy of Mariposa County Museum)

answer, he stocked up on picks, shovels, and other equipment the miners might need. Then he went to San Francisco and walked the streets waving a bottle of gold and yelling, "GOLD! GOLD FROM THE AMERICAN RIVER!" The news spread like wildfire!

Sure enough, people quickly began arriving at Brannan's store and the mill. Marshall said:

> *"With pans, shovels, and hoes, all anxious to fall to work and dig up our mill. As fast as one party disappeared, another would arrive. I had the greatest kind of trouble to get rid of them."*[4]

He sent them off in all directions:

> *"I told them to go to such and such a places, because it appeared that they would dig nowhere but in such places as I pointed out. Thus in a very short time we discovered that the whole country was but one bed of gold."*[5]

As word of the discoveries spread through Northern California, almost everyone who was able to dig set out for Sutter's Mill. Before the gold discovery there were about 800 people living in the town of San Francisco. After the discovery fewer than 100 people were left!

The first published announcement of the discovery was made on March 15, 1848, in the San Francisco newspaper *The Californian*. The gold at Sutter's Mill was no longer just California news because people in other states and countries read the newspaper. Soon the whole world found out where the riches were, and hundreds of thousands of people decided to come to California for gold.

Miners at the Esmeralda Camp during the gold rush era. (Courtesy of Arizona Department of Mines and Geology)

THE "49ERS"

The first ships carrying gold seekers from outside California arrived in San Francisco on February 28, 1849. Because these fortune hunters arrived in 1849, they were called "49ers." They were soon followed by thousands of others. In 1848 there were about 5,000 men digging in the mountains. In 1849 more than 100,000 came to California to dig gold. Most of the "49ers" were young men, some even in their teens with little or no knowledge of mining.

MINER'S LAW

What made the California gold rush unique is that it was a "poor man's" gold rush. For the first time in history, the gold was there for everyone to find, not just for some king or government. During the first years there were few, if any, rules—only "Miner's Law." A man could dig where he wanted, as much as he wanted, when he wanted . . . and keep everything he found.

A miner could dig on someone else's land or even in town and could **stake a claim** anywhere he found gold. To stake a claim all he had to do was mark out the area he wanted (usually with wooden stakes) and that patch of ground was his as long as he worked on it.

The miners had their own court system to handle disputes. They would form a jury and decide who was right. If a man was found guilty of a crime, the worst punishment given was forcing him to leave the diggings. No miner wanted that!

The gold was so plentiful in the first years of the rush that there was very little crime in the mines. A man could leave his tools on his claim and know they'd still be there when he returned. Miners didn't steal each other's gold or each other's claims. It was a great time in history.

Some amazing finds were made the first year. A nugget weighing 1,200 ounces (34 kilograms) was found in Woods Creek and another weighing 400 ounces (11 kilograms) was taken from the Mokelumne River. Gold production in 1848 was about $240,000. In 1849 it jumped to over $10 million dollars. By 1852 gold production reached the all-time high of over $81 million dollars. In 1854 the largest nugget of gold ever found in California was discovered at Carson Hill—it weighed over 3,000 ounces (88 kilograms)!

NOT EVERYONE FINDS THEIR FORTUNE

The gold rush was not all peaches and cream, however. Sutter, who was part of the first gold discovery, was also one of the rush's first casualties. He tried to gain control of the Sutter's Mill gold fields by signing a treaty with the Yalesumni Indians giving him the rights to the land. The U.S. military governor Richard B. Mason, refused to sign the treaty, however, because Sutter was originally given the land by Mexico. Mason argued that Mexican land grants no longer counted in the new state of California.

Sutter then tried persuading the Yalesumni Indians to mine the gold for him, but he was unsuccessful. In the end, Sutter was overwhelmed by the swarms of men rushing to the gold fields. At first he tried to help them but the number of men quickly became too great.

On May 23, 1848 he wrote in his diary, *"Hosts arriving by water and land heading for the mountains. Fine day."* Two days later he wrote, *"Great hosts continue to the Mts."*[6]

The town of Gold Run, Placer County, in the late 1800s. (Courtesy of Placer County Chamber of Commerce)

These were the last words he would ever write in his diary. The miners rushing to the mountains overran his fields and scattered his horses and cattle. Sutter's dream of having his own fortune was trampled, but other men's dreams were just beginning.

HOW THE CAMPS GOT THEIR NAMES

As men rushed from one gold discovery to another, camps and towns sprang up all over California. Coloma, the site of Sutter's Mill, grew from a mill camp of about 10 men to a town of 4,000 in just one year. Most of the mining camps were named after the group of miners who first discovered gold there: Iowa Hill, Wisconsin Hill, Michigan Bluff, Illinoistown, Frenchmen's Flat, Dutch Flat, Chinese Camp, Chili Gulch, and Kanaka Flat.

Other camps were named for things that happened there: Grizzly Flat, Rattlesnake Bar, Loafer Hill, Cut

Gold rush ghost town. (Courtesy of M. Broman)

Throat, and Fiddletown. The miners gave some camps funny names: Hum Bug, Poverty Flat, Poorman's Bar and Hog Eye.

GHOST TOWNS

The towns that sprung up during the gold rush were usually built quickly with poor materials. When the gold ran out, or when new gold was discovered elsewhere, the miners left town. The empty streets and buildings left behind became "**ghost towns**." When the miners talked about one of those deserted towns they would say "Only ghosts live there now."

Some of the best descriptions we have of these early camps are found in the "Shirley Letters." Mrs. Louise Clappe (known as "Dame Shirley") arrived at

Gold' rush ghost town. (Courtesy of M. Broman)

Rich Bar in the summer of 1851 and wrote letters to her sister about the camp.

She described the Empire Hotel, where she first stayed, as the only two-story building in the camp. It was built of rough planks, with a piece of canvas for a roof. It had the only three glass windows in camp, and doors made of blue cloth hung from leather hinges. "*It is just such a piece of carpentering as a child of two years, gifted with the strength of a man, would produce, if it wanted to play at making grown up houses.*"[7]

She said by the following winter, Rich Bar was a ghost town.

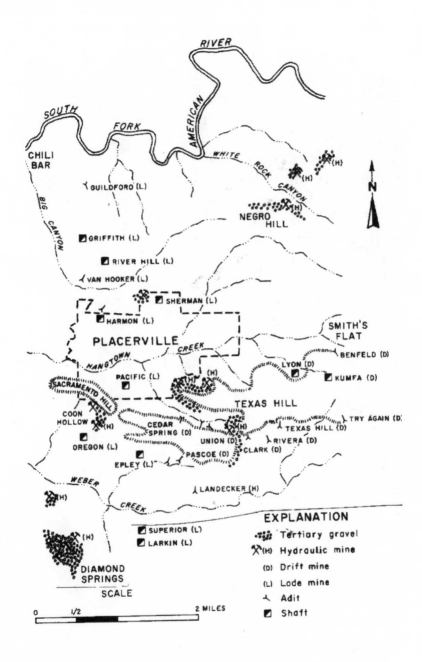

Map of Placerville showing locations of mines and camps. (Courtesy of California Division of Mines and Geology)

The men came by the thousands: in wagons, by ship, and even on foot. Most planned to strike it rich and return home. Some did return, but many more stayed and populated the land. As a result, California emerged from the turmoil of the rush to become the most important Western state. These California settlements made the West more appealing to other pioneers.

By 1855 the California rush was over, but gold mining continues even today. Miners from California went on to make other gold discoveries in places like Colorado, Nevada, Alaska and Canada's Fraser River, in the area that is now British Columbia.

THE PEOPLE WHO RUSHED FOR GOLD

At the start of the gold rush, most of the miners were from other U.S. states and were new to California. They quickly made the state their home and everyone who came after them was seen as a "foreigner." These first U.S. miners, however, weren't the only people who took part in the gold rush. Women, children and men from all over the world tried their hands at striking it rich.

KIDS IN THE CAMPS

There were few children in the gold camps in the early days, because the journey west was very dangerous for children. Also, each miner wanted to be the first to get to the gold, so they left behind anything that would slow them down.

The small number of children in the camps made them very popular entertainers. The most famous child

Young miner in the 1800s. (Courtesy of Utah State Historical Society)

star was Lotta Crabtree. When Lotta's father failed to strike it rich as a gold miner, her mother put her on stage as a dancer. She was an instant success and toured the camps for several years before going on to worldwide fame. When Lotta died years later, this poor miner's daughter left behind a fortune of four million dollars!

WOMEN IN THE CAMPS

There were only about two women for every 100 men in California in 1849. When a woman arrived in camp,

End of a work shift in the mines, circa 1900. (Courtesy of California Division of Mines and Geology).

the men stopped working to see the amazing sight, and brought her gold nuggets or wildflowers as gifts.

The first women to come to the gold fields were miners' wives or entertainers, but some women disguised themselves as men and worked as miners. They were called "**Madame Pantaloons**" by the other miners.

Lola Montez was a famous woman of the gold rush. She toured the camps as a popular dancer, then bought

part of a mine in Grass Valley. She settled there with
her pet monkeys and a tame grizzly bear.

Eleanor Dumont was a well-known gambler of the
gold rush era. People in Nevada City were shocked
when Eleanor opened a gambling house only three days
after arriving in town. The miners had to mind their
manners in her place—no swearing or getting drunk
was allowed.

Mary Ellen Pleasant was a freed slave who came to
the gold rush as a cook. She made enough money in the
California mining camps to open a boardinghouse for
the miners. She was a great success and used her money
to help other African Americans.

NATIVE AMERICANS

The Native American people of California suffered the
most and benefited the least from the gold rush. Because
they believed that people could not own parts of the
Earth, they were never very interested in the gold or in
mining it. Even when they did join in the mining, they
were soon forced out of the diggings by white miners.

California tribes such as the Yalesumni, Miwok and
Nisenan were pushed farther and farther away from
their homelands. Usually the miners organized themselves to fight the native tribes and take their land, but
sometimes the U.S. military even joined in. When the
tribes tried to fight back, they were overwhelmed by the
number of the miners and their weapons. Tragically,
some of the tribes were completely wiped out.

There is a wonderful movie and many interesting
books about "Ishi", the last surviving member of the
Yahi tribe, who was discovered in northern California
in 1911.

MEXICAN MINERS

Mexican miners were some of the first, and most skilled, miners to rush to California when gold was discovered. They were also the largest group of foreign miners. Many came from Sonora, Mexico and established a camp in northern California called Sonora, which is a town today.

Unfortunately, the white miners often discriminated against the Mexican miners. One Mexican miner who got tired of the unfair treatment was Joaquin Murietta. He became a bandit after his cabin was robbed, his wife and brother were murdered, and his gold was stolen. He was the most famous bandit in California history. When he disappeared, some said that Murietta returned to Mexico with his loot and lived a long life. Others believed that he was killed by a group of Rangers (as California law officers were called during that time), who claimed a $1,000 reward for his head.

CHILEAN MINERS

The gold-seekers from Chile were the second largest group of foreign miners. Most of the Chileans were highly-educated men from prominent families. They were experienced miners and knew how to find gold. This led to a lot of jealousy and conflict with the white miners. The conflict even turned into the "Chili Gulch War" of 1849. Several miners were shot and prisoners were taken by both sides.

AFRICAN AMERICANS

Most of the African Americans in the gold rush were runaway slaves or slaves brought to the mines by south-

Children in a mining camp with vendor. (Courtesy of Title Insurance
and Trust Company)

erners. The most famous African American of this time was Jim Beckwourth, a former trapper, guide and mountain man. He found gold on the Stanislaus River and later ran a trading post in Sonora. Beckwourth Pass in northern California is named for him.

There was a large settlement of nearly 100 freed slaves near Grass Valley. They weren't particularly interested in working the mines, but they held many jobs in the camps and were an important part of that community.

JEWISH PEOPLE

Jewish people helped establish some of the most successful early mining companies. They also opened stores in the camps and were a big part of turning those mining camps into today's cities, instead of letting them become ghost towns.

The most famous Jewish man of the gold rush was Levi Strauss, who arrived in California in 1850. When a miner complained that no clothes could hold up under the rough wear and tear of mining, Mr. Strauss made him a pair of pants out of tent canvas. They wore so well, soon other miners wanted a pair of "Levi's pants."

Some say Strauss used the sails from the abandoned ships in San Francisco Bay to make the pants until he could get blue denim, which was easier to sew. The Levi's™ jeans people wear today were born during the California gold rush!

IRISH MINERS

The Irish were some of the first miners to arrive in the gold fields. They were some of the first politicians in the gold camps and built many of the camps' first churches.

Chinese miner with rocker and other tools. (Courtesy of California Division of Mines and Geology)

HAWAIIAN MINERS

The Kanakas were from the Hawaiian Islands and mined in California in the early part of the gold rush. They were also discriminated against and often robbed of their claims by the white miners. There is a creek in Sierra County which bears their name and still produces gold today.

CHINESE MINERS

According to historians there were only seven Chinese people in California when the discovery was made at Sutter's Mill. By 1852 there were 25,000. Many of the surviving gold rush towns still have old Chinese buildings.

Some Chinese people worked as laborers and merchants in the camps, but most worked in the diggings. They were another group that suffered from a great deal of discrimination by the white miners. Most often they were only allowed to dig in areas that white miners

thought were worthless. If they did find gold, they were usually chased off their claim by a white miner.

FRENCH MINERS

There is no doubt that the French were very active in the gold rush. There were two French Bars, four French Camps, four French Gulches, two French Flats, two French Hills, a French Corral, a Frenchman's Bar and a French-town among the camps and diggings. By 1853 it is estimated that there were 30,000 French people in California.

GOLD RUSH CELEBRITIES

Some people who originally came to California in search of gold, "struck it rich" in unexpected ways. They are now famous for different reasons.

John C. Fremont's home in Mariposa, California, circa 1860. (Courtesy of Mariposa County Museum)

John C. Fremont purchased California land in 1847 that had enough gold on it to make him wealthy. He was one of the new state's first U.S. Senators and in 1856 he ran for President, losing to James Buchanan.

Kit Carson scouted with Fremont. He is credited with the discovery of the first **lode gold mine** (a vein of gold ore mined either through a shaft or a tunnel) in Mariposa County, in 1849.

Mark Twain, one of the most famous writers of the U.S., tried his luck as a miner for a short time without success. He then wrote the most popular story about the gold miners, "The Celebrated Jumping Frog of Calaveras County." The town where the story takes place, Angel's Camp, still holds a frog-jumping contest every year.

Bret Harte was also a great American writer. He came to California in 1854, and his stories of life in the mining camps such as "The Outcasts of Poker Flats" and

"The Luck of Roaring Camp" are classics of American literature.

George Hearst came to the mines from a small farm in Missouri. He made his fortune in mining and became a U.S. Senator. The Hearst family is still one of the richest families in the U.S. today.

John Studebaker came from Indiana in 1853 to dig for gold. He ended up making wheelbarrows for the miners and earned enough money to return home and open a factory to build wagons. Later he built the automobiles that bear his name.

Philip D. Armour also came to California to mine gold, but ended up selling meat to the miners. He later started the Armour Meat Packing Company, which still makes food today.

Leland Stanford arrived in California in 1852 and opened a store. He went on to become Governor and a U.S. Senator. Using the money he made from the gold rush, he founded Stanford University.

The "Big Four" (Leland Stanford, Mark Hopkins, Collis Huntington and Charles Crocker) used their mining riches to build California's first railroad.

IT'S NOT JUST
IN CALIFORNIA

California isn't the only place where people started a huge commotion looking for gold. Many areas around the United States and the world were changed by their own gold rushes.

THE AUSTRALIAN GOLD RUSH

E. H. Hargraves came to California in the rush of 1849. He noticed that the gold fields of California looked very similar to his home country of Australia. He returned to Australia and began prospecting at once. He soon discovered lots of gold around Melbourne and Sydney. This started the great Australian gold rush of 1851. Over a million people came to Australia over the next four years.

The Australian rush was unique because there were many large nuggets discovered by the miners. One miner named B.J. Holtermann found a mass of gold that was five feet tall, two feet wide and three inches thick! Two prospectors digging their wagon out of the mud found a nugget weighing 2,300 ounces (65 kilograms).

The development of electric gold detectors has sparked a new rush to Australia. In the early 1990s, a nugget worth over a million dollars was found there with a metal detector. The "Hand of Faith" nugget, as it is called, was buried only 6 inches under the ground!

THE CANADIAN GOLD RUSHES

The first large group of "49ers" to leave California went to Canada's Fraser River, in what is now British Columbia. In 1858, a miner named James Douglas shipped 800 ounces (23 kilograms) of gold from Victoria, British Columbia, to the U.S. Mint in San Francisco. The arrival of this gold started the rush. In just a few months the population of Victoria grew from about 200 people to 30,000 people.

The first miners to arrive found gold at the mouth of the Fraser River, and then they hit the jackpot about 100 miles north, at Hill's Bar. This area produced over two million dollars in gold.

The next big strike in Canada was on Antler Creek, near the Cariboo Mountains of British Columbia. Then came the discoveries on Williams Creek, where one miner found 96 ounces (3 kilograms) of gold in *one* pan full of dirt! By the late 1860s, over $100 million dollars worth of gold had been discovered in the Cariboo area.

The rush to the gold fields of the Yukon and the Canadian northwest began in 1896. The area's first gold came from the Yukon and Klondike rivers and the Quartz and Bonanza creeks.

For some California miners, the gold rushes to Canada were a disappointment. Some areas were difficult to work because of snow and flooded rivers, and there was less gold to be found than in California. There were also more fees and rules for mining in Canada than the U.S. miners were used to. These miners were used to a wild, free life and many returned to California as quickly as they could.

THE COLORADO GOLD RUSH

In the 1850s, a prospector named George Jackson struck gold in what is now the state of Colorado. Using a tin cup and a hunting knife, he dug out a few spoonfuls of gold worth about $10. The ground was so frozen that he had to build a fire to thaw it before he could dig. Word of the gold soon leaked out and the rush to Colorado began.

At the time of the discoveries, Auraria was a camp of about 20 tents. It later became the city of Denver. By 1870 Colorado had replaced California as the largest gold producing state.

There was a second rush to Colorado in the early 1890s. A prospector named Bob Womack spent nearly 12 years looking for gold in Cripple Creek. Once, when he was drunk, he sold his claim for $300. It went on to produce three million dollars for its new owners. Maybe that's why they called him "Crazy Bob." Cripple Creek is probably the richest gold area ever discovered in the United States. In an area only 6 miles square, $340 million dollars worth of gold was found in just 25 years.

THE MONTANA GOLD RUSH

The number of miners who went to Montana was small

compared to other rushes, but the amount of gold, silver and copper found was very large. The first discoveries were made by three brothers named Stuart, from the California gold rush, who wandered into Montana's Deer Lodge Valley in 1858. They found **color** (the pieces of gold left in the pan after panning) in what became known as Gold Creek.

The brothers were driven out of the area by the Black-feet Indians and it wasn't until 1860 that they were able to return to the creek. Soon gold was found in other creeks too. Between 1862 and 1900 more than $300 million dollars worth of gold was produced by Montana mines.

But gold wasn't the only treasure of the state. Copper and silver produced the *real* wealth. By 1950, Montana's mines had produced nearly two billion dollars worth of copper.

THE BLACK HILLS GOLD RUSH

Wild Bill Hickok

Some of the most famous people in Western American history were part of the rush to the Black Hills, in what is now the state of South Dakota. George Custer, Wild Bill Hickok, Calamity Jane, Deadwood Dick and George Hearst were among those who went to the Black Hills because of the gold.

This gold rush is also responsible for one of the saddest pages in American history. The Black Hills were, and still are, a holy place of deep spiritual meaning to the Native Americans of the area.

In 1868 the United
States signed a treaty with
the Sioux Indians, which
gave the tribe the Black
Hills forever. This treaty
didn't keep prospectors
from trying to find out if
the rumors of gold in the
hills were true. At first the
U.S. army kept the fortune
hunters out of the Native
American land, but the
miners kept pressuring the
government to open the
hills for exploration.

George Armstrong Custer

In 1874, the army
sent Custer and a large troop of soldiers into the Black
Hills. He also took several miners with him and they
discovered gold. The government then tried to buy the
land back from the Sioux, but they refused to sell. A fight
broke out and, in the end, the Sioux were forced to give
up their sacred land. Two years later, Custer and 264 soldiers were killed by the Sioux in the battle of Little Big
Horn, in Montana.

In 1875 there were about 50 miners in the area of
Deadwood Creek, South Dakota, but by 1877 there
were over 7,000 men searching for gold in the creeks
and gulches.

In 1876, two brothers named Fred and Moses
Manuel discovered one of the richest mines in the world,
the Homestake Mine. They sold their mine to George
Hearst for $70,000. The Homestake Mining Company is
still operating today and has produced nearly one billion
dollars worth of gold!

THE ALASKA GOLD RUSH

The Alaska gold rush is considered the last great western gold rush. It began in 1896, when small amounts of gold were discovered on the Klondike River by a miner named Robert Henderson. Gold was soon found in other areas of Alaska, but the areas were so far from civilization that it took a long time for the news to reach the rest of the United States.

When boats arrived in Seattle in 1897 carrying Alaskan miners with gold, the rush began. 100,000 men rushed to the new diggings, but it was very difficult to get to the remote areas containing gold. Only about 40,000 of the 100,000 gold-seekers actually reached the gold.

NEVADA'S SILVER RUSH

With all the digging the miners did, it was only natural for them to discover many treasures besides gold. One of the most profitable finds, other than gold, was silver.

Just over the mountains from the California gold fields, in Nevada, a few miners were happy to scratch out just enough gold to feed themselves. One of the miners, Henry Comstock, was thought of as lazy and not very bright. One day in 1854, he and a few other men were digging for gold, but they were having problems with the "blue muck" that kept clogging up their sluice boxes.

They later discovered that the "blue muck" was actually silver. The men, who were more interested in gold, sold their claims for very little money and ended up with nothing. The men who bought the claims, including George Hearst, became very rich. The Comstock Lode, as it is called, became the richest silver mining area ever known.

While the city of Reno, Nevada was not a mining town, it was founded during the silver rush because there were so many miners settling in the state. Reno began when W.C. Fuller built a ferry across the Truckee River. Later, the ferry site became a train stop, and the town continued to grow from there.

From the first discovery of rich deposits in California to the last big discovery in the wilds of Alaska, the gold rush period in the United States lasted for about 50 years. There have been other recent, smaller gold rushes to South America and Nevada, but nothing like the rushes of the 1800s. The great rushes may be over, but there is still A LOT of gold waiting to be found. Now it's *your* turn to go out and seek your fortune!

CHAPTER

HOW TO PROSPECT AND FIND GOLD

WARNING!!! DO NOT PROSPECT ALONE!

The areas where you search for gold—rivers, mountains, canyons—can be dangerous. Always go with an adult, in case of an accident. Get your family to join you and maybe they will strike it rich too! Great discoveries are even better when they are shared.

PICKING YOUR SPOT

The first thing you need to do is find an area near you where gold has been discovered before. Early prospectors dug into and checked out most of the mountains, canyons, streams, creeks and rivers of North America searching for gold. Take advantage of what they learned.

If there hasn't been much gold found in your area, don't despair. You could always be the first person to

Old miner panning. (Courtesy of Los Angeles County Museum)

discover it. You might also try prospecting in other gold areas when you're traveling on vacation. Maybe you could even talk your family into a "prospecting trip."

If people have discovered gold in your state (see Chapter 9) you should get more detailed information about the areas where it has been found. The librarian at your library can help you locate books or articles about gold mining in your state. Study these and pinpoint the area you want to search. The closest area with gold may not be the best place for you to prospect. You want to find a placer mining area at first because it is the easiest way for a new miner (you) to find gold.

There may be a treasure hunting/prospecting supply store in your area, or close to an area you want to prospect in. These stores will have lots of books and pamphlets on prospecting and the people there will be able to tell you the places that local miners are finding the most gold today. They can also tell you about clubs or groups in your area who go prospecting.

Read everything you can about the area you want to prospect, including exactly which parts have produced the most gold. Once you have learned all that you can, you're ready to go!

DON'T FORGET YOUR TREASURE MAP

A good map is a prospector's best friend. Your state's Department of Mines and Geology (see Chapter 9) should have maps showing the mineral deposits in your state. You can get topographical ("topo" for short) maps at an outdoor supply store or a map store. Topo maps will show details like hills, valleys, mine sites and large **tailing piles.**

Tailing piles are the rocks left behind after the gold has been removed by earlier miners. These piles are good places to start hunting because you know gold has probably been found there before, and some may have been missed. Studying your maps and planning your search will make your trip more exciting. And if you plan, you're more likely to hit the jackpot.

Tailing piles. (Courtesy of James Klein)

WHERE TO FIND THE GOLD

When **ore** (rock that holds minerals) with gold in it reaches the surface of the earth, it forms an **outcropping**. The outcropping of ore is then worn away by water, wind, heat and cold.

Gold is tougher than the ore that holds it, so when the ore breaks up and is carried away, the gold is released and left behind. If the outcropping is on the side of a hill or canyon, the heavy gold will move downhill in rain or wind.

Once the gold reaches a stream it gets picked up in the current and carried until something (like a big rock or tree) stops it. The gold is also left behind when the stream slows down through a curve or where it widens.

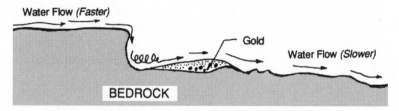

Anything that slows the stream's flow may cause the water to drop heavy gold particles. Look around the base of a drop-off in a streambed for gold.

Because gold is heavier than other rock, when it stops moving it will work its way down through layers of loose rock and silt, until it reaches a solid rock layer called **bedrock**.

After gold has worked its way to the bottom of the stream, it is difficult for the stream to pick it back up again. Over time gold builds up in these places, creating a **placer deposit**. These are the places you want to search for.

WHERE TO LOOK IN A STREAM

You should always have an adult with you when you're prospecting—especially in or around streams. There is actually no reason for you to get into the stream to find gold. You can easily pan and work a sluice box from the edge of the stream. The best places to dig along a streambed are:

★ the inside of a curve in the stream

★ downstream from boulders and sand bars

★ places were there is an eddy

★ any fault or shelf line crossing the stream

★ places where the stream widens and the water
slows down

★ downstream from any natural dam (like a log) that
causes a pool to form

★ around the roots of trees on the stream bank

Other heavy minerals may be found with gold in
the placer deposits. Magnetite (also called "black sand")
is almost always found, but garnets, zircon, hematite,
chromate, platinum, cinnabar, tungsten minerals, tita-
nium minerals, pyrite, and even diamonds have also
been found with gold! If you would like to know what
these gems and minerals look like, your library should
have a gem and mineral guide book with color photos
of each of the gems and minerals listed.

Gold is soft and gets hammered by rocks as it tum-
bles along in the stream. Pieces you find with edges that
are either round or flat have probably been in the stream

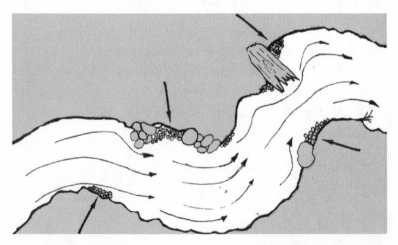

Gold deposits may be hiding inside the curves of a stream and around
rocks or fallen trees.

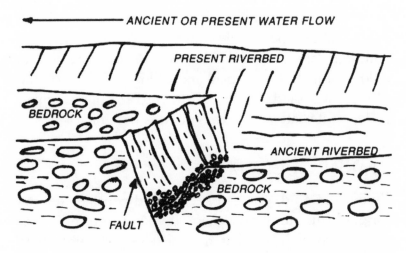

Cross-section of a river showing a pocket in the riverbed which traps gold, gravel, sand and silt.

for a longer period of time than the pieces that are still in their original crystalline form. Crystalline nuggets are known as "**coarse gold**" and probably haven't traveled far from their outcropping. You may be able to find the outcropping, and more gold, close by.

Don't forget to check the canyon walls where they have been cut by the stream. The stream was up there once and gold deposits may be left behind. Fill your bucket with dirt from there, bring it down to the stream and pan it out or run it through your sluice box.

Once you dig your dirt, it's time to get the gold out of it. Read the next chapter for how to pan it out and use a sluice box.

DON'T BE FOOLED BY "FOOL'S GOLD"

You may find lots of bright, shiny flakes in your pan, but not all of them are gold. Sometimes you'll be fooled by iron pyrite, which prospectors call "fool's gold." There are several ways to tell fool's gold from real gold. Fool's gold is cube shaped, while gold is more likely to be round and irregularly shaped. Fool's gold also weighs less than gold, will float in your pan, and will normally be on top of the black sand. Finally, try to cut the mineral with a knife—if it shatters or breaks up, it is not gold.

STAKING A CLAIM

If you find gold, you can keep it and continue mining for gold without filing a claim. If you want to have that area to yourself, so that no one else can mine there while you look for gold on it, you should file a claim to the land. You should only file a claim if you think there is a lot of gold there. The law says that kids can file claims by themselves, but I highly recommend that you have a parent or guardian help you.

To file a claim, go to the County Recorders Office in the area you discovered your gold (you can get the address and phone number from a local phone book). They will give you the right forms and tell you what you need to do to file the claim.

WHAT TO DO WITH YOUR GOLD ONCE YOU FIND IT

Most people save their gold and display it at home or in shows. If you find a lot of gold and want to cash it in, there are many places that will buy it from you: jewelry stores, refineries, assayers, mining or prospecting stores, or even your dentist may want to buy the gold from you.

The price of gold changes every day. The daily price of gold is called the **spot price**. You should check the spot price for gold in your newspaper the same day

Hydraulic mining in the 1800s. (Courtesy of Placer County Chamber of Commerce)

you're going to sell your gold, so you know what the gold is worth.

LEAVE IT AS YOU FOUND IT: PROTECTING NATURE

One of the great things about prospecting is that you get to wander in beautiful mountains and along streams, and find gold while you're at it. It is very important that you take care of this wilderness, so others can enjoy it too.

Unfortunately, several kinds of mining have been very destructive to the environment. Hydraulic mining was banned in the 1880s because it destroyed so much nature. Giant hoses were used to wash away whole mountainsides. Scars left by this kind of mining can still be seen in some mining areas.

Strip mining uses bulldozers to remove dirt, trees, rocks and anything else covering gold or other minerals. Laws now require operators to return the land back to its original condition when they've finished mining an area.

Toxic chemicals have also been used to remove gold from rock. These chemicals leak into the water in the area, poisoning plants, fish and other animals. Strict laws now control their use.

One person, like you, searching for gold and panning in streams, can protect nature with just a little effort. Most holes that you make in stream beds when you're panning or sluicing will be filled back in the next time it rains. Still, it is a good idea to fill your holes in when you're done digging in an area.

Clean up after yourself and carry out any trash you find while you're prospecting. Leave the wilderness just as you found it, or even improve it if you can.

THE GOLD GEAR
YOU WILL NEED

The only tools you *really* need to find gold are a shovel and a gold pan, just like the early miners used. The other equipment is optional and will just help you be a better prospector.

You may be able to find or make some of these items at home, while others you can buy at prospecting and treasure hunting stores.

Young prospector panning for gold. (Courtesy of James Klein)

GOLD PAN

From beginners to old pros, every prospector has a gold pan. During the California gold rush, some miners cooked and panned for gold with the same pan because they only had one!

Kids dig for gold by the river. (Courtesy of Tee Dee Company)

There are several sizes and kinds of pans available today—steel, copper or plastic. I suggest the 12–14 inch plastic pan because:

★ the color of the plastic pan—black or dark green—is best to see gold against

★ they have **riffles** built in to help trap the heavier materials, like gold (riffles are little ridges that catch the heavier minerals)

★ they are much lighter than steel pans

★ a pan smaller than 12 inches across won't hold enough material, while a bigger one will take too long to work.

PANNING IT OUT

❶ Find a place in the stream where the water is deep enough to put your pan completely under the water, and where it's running just fast enough to carry off the muddy water you will create. You need the water to be clear so you can see what you're doing. Try to find a spot with a rock to sit on. It's a lot more comfortable to sit down.

❷ Fill your pan about two-thirds full with the dirt you want to wash. Never fill your pan all the way because it will be too heavy and will take too long to pan. Put your pan completely under the water and use your fingers to stir up the dirt. This will get out floating material like leaves and twigs.

Step 2: Fill your pan about ⅔ full with dirt. (Courtesy of Keene Engineering)

❸ Remove all the larger rocks you can see in the pan. Be sure to wash any dirt clinging to the rocks back into the pan. Stir up the gravel again and continue removing any other rocks you find.

Step 3: Remove any large rocks from the pan. (Courtesy of Keene Engineering)

❹ Shake the pan from side to side to help settle

the heavier material to the bottom. You can shake it pretty hard, as long as you don't throw any of the gravel out. Again remove any large rocks or pebbles you can see.

5 Swirl the material around in the pan using a circular motion, always keeping your pan under water. This will cause the

Step 4: Shake the pan to settle the heavier material to the bottom. (Courtesy of Keene Engineering)

lighter gravel to come to the surface and the heavier minerals and gravel to sink to the bottom of the pan.

You should now see the lighter sands and gravel on the surface. Tilt your pan forward as you rotate it and wash the lighter material out over the edge. Make sure the riffles are at the front of the pan and the material is washing out over them. Repeat this process until only a

small amount of lighter material remains with the black sands.

6 Now comes the good part. Take your pan out of the stream leaving about an inch of water covering the material. Swirl the material around. If you can see any pieces of gold, take them out.

Step 6: Tilt the pan forward allowing the lighter gravel to wash back into the river. (Courtesy of Keene Engineering)

Amount of gold found in one day. (Courtesy of Keene Engineering)

Place the pan back under the water and carefully wash out any more of the lighter sand and gravel left in the pan. Again, lift out the pan leaving an inch of water in it. Tilt the pan and shake your heavier materials into one side of the pan. When all the black sand is on one side, give the pan a couple more good shakes.

Now begin swirling the water over the sand, removing a top layer each time. If you're lucky, you will begin seeing the gold in the black sand. Shake the pan again and work the flakes down to the bottom. Continue swirling and keep washing off the top layers until just the gold remains.

Remove the gold from your pan and go get some more dirt to wash. You are now a gold miner!

(Courtesy of Keene Engineering)

PRACTICE PANNING AT HOME

Be sure you ask your parents' permission before you practice panning at home. It can be messy, so clean up after yourself. Your parents may want you to practice outside instead of inside.

All you need is a gold pan or even a pie pan, a bathtub (or any large tub), a little sand, and some brass B.B.s (shiny brass tacks or buttons would also work, but not as well). Fill the tub with water and fill the pan ½ full with the sand. Take six B.B.s and put them on top of the sand.

Spread them around in a circle, then push them down in the sand and cover them. Start with step 4 above and pan out the B.B.s. Keep practicing until every time you put six B.B.s in the sand, you get six B.B.s in your pan after panning it out. With a little practice you'll be an old pro before you ever go searching for real gold.

SHOVEL

A shovel is the second most important tool a prospector needs. You can use a long-handled shovel, which is easier for your back, or a short-handled one, which is easier to carry.

SMALL BOTTLE

A small, clear bottle is perfect to hold any gold you find while prospecting. Plastic is best because it won't break if you drop it.

BUCKET

A bucket is great for carrying equipment in and out of your prospecting site. Also, you can use it to carry material from dry areas to a stream to pan it. Any bucket will do, but a metal bucket will last longer. The size depends on how much you want to carry.

TROWEL

A small garden trowel is handy to reach into difficult places like tree roots and crevices.

TWEEZERS

A pair of tweezers will help you remove the smallest pieces of gold and gems from your pan.

SPOON

An old spoon works well to clean out the very small cracks and crevices you find.

MAGNIFYING GLASS

A small magnifying glass helps to examine rocks for minerals. You can also use it to check out the small pieces of minerals in your pan.

(Courtesy of Keene Engineering)

BRUSH

A small paintbrush can be used to clean out cracks and crevices that may contain gold.

COMPASS

It can be easy to get lost while you're out prospecting,

even with an adult. A compass can help you find your way back if you know how to use it.

PROSPECTOR'S HAMMER

The prospector's hammer is flat on one end and pointed on the other. You use it to split rocks open to see if they contain any valuable minerals and also as a pick in areas that are hard to reach.

(Courtesy of Keene Engineering)

After you've been prospecting for a while, you may want to get some of the items listed below. You don't need them to find gold, but experienced miners often use them to find even more gold.

SLUICE BOX

The more dirt you wash, the more gold you get. With a sluice box you can wash five to ten times more gravel than you can pan in a day. When you put a sluice box in a stream, it uses the flowing water to separate the gold from the dirt and gravel. The sluice traps

(Courtesy of Keene Engineering)

the gold behind riffles in the bottom of the box. It is a simple device that you can buy (even kid-sized sluices) or make yourself.

Most sluices are made of lightweight metal and come with a removable riffle tray. The riffle tray sits on top of a carpet that traps the really small pieces of gold.

When it's time to clean out your sluice box, just pull out the riffle tray and rinse the carpet in your bucket. The material that got caught in the carpet will then be in your bucket for you to pan out.

HOW TO WORK A SLUICE

Pick your location, and then set up your sluice box in the stream as close as possible to the gravel. Put your box in a place where the current is strong enough to move the material through the sluice and just deep enough to almost reach the top of your sluice box. The water should be flowing fast enough to carry lighter gravel material through the sluice and out the end, and leave heavier material behind.

Scoop or shovel material directly into the front of the sluice box, but be careful not to overload the box

Sluicing for gold. (Courtesy of Tee Dee Company)

because this will cause you to lose gold. You should feed it just fast enough that the top edges of the riffles are visible at all times.

Remove rocks and other material that may build up and clog the "out" end of your sluice. Don't put large rocks into the sluice because they will cut your water flow and knock your gold out of the riffles.

When you can see a large build-up of black sand on your riffles it's time to clean out your sluice box. Lift your sluice out of the water, being careful not to lose any **concentrates** (the black sands and gold left in a pan or behind the riffles after the lighter material has been washed away). Then dump the concentrates into your bucket. Now you're ready to pan out the gold!

BUILD YOUR OWN SLUICE

Making your own sluice box is pretty simple. It's basically a trough with obstructions in the bottom to trap the heavier materials like gold. For the bottom, you need one piece of wood, 10 or 12 inches wide, 1 inch thick and as long as you want it. For the sides, you need two pieces of wood, 6 inches high, 1 inch thick and the same length as the bottom. Last, you need several one inch square pieces of wood cut as wide as your bottom piece. Nail the square pieces, five to six inches apart, all along the bottom of the board—these are your riffles. Then nail the side boards to the bottom and you have yourself a sluice box.

METAL DETECTORS

The old miners didn't have metal detectors, but many miners today use them. The old metal detectors couldn't

Derrick Jensen with metal detector. (Courtesy of Fisher Research Laboratory)

separate the good beeps (for gold, silver, etc.) from the bad (for iron, bottle caps, etc.) and you had to dig at every beep, when most of the time it was junk. Now there are metal detectors just for gold. The new "electronic prospectors," as I call them, or "nugget shooters," as they call themselves, are doing quite well today.

Some huge nuggets have been found with detectors. The "Hand of Faith" nugget was discovered in Australia with a metal detector. It is worth over one million dollars and was buried only six inches underground!

Casey Carver, a seven-year-old Australian boy, was prospecting with a gold detector when he found a seven-ounce (200-gram) gold nugget!

OTHER EQUIPMENT MINERS USE

The rocker is a primitive kind of sluice box that is shaped like a cradle with rockers on each end.

The dredge is just a sluice box with a vacuum hose attached to suck up gravel from the bottom of streams. It works like your vacuum cleaner, but uses water to suck up the material.

The dry washer is also like a sluice box, but it uses air to separate the gold and other heavy minerals from the sands and gravel. It's used in areas without much water, such as deserts.

C H A P T E R

9

WHERE TO FIND GOLD NEAR YOU

OFF-LIMITS VERSUS A-OK

There are many places for you to strike it rich out there. Here's where you *can* prospect for gold:

★ Most Bureau of Land Management (BLM) and National Forest lands in the western United States are open to prospecting, mining and staking claims.

★ Some areas of Forest Service land are open for "recreational mining," but don't allow people to stake claims. Recreational miners are people who are not full-time miners, but like to spend their free time looking for gold.

★ Usually you can prospect on private land if you ask the owner's permission first.

★ Many historic mining spots, like Sutter's Mill, encourage visitors to pan on their land.

Here's where you *can't* prospect for gold:

★ National Parks

★ Indian Reservations

★ State-owned land

★ City-owned land

★ County-owned land

★ Private land (unless you get permission)

★ Military land

★ Permanent lake beds

★ Reservoirs

★ National Monuments

★ State Monuments

★ Any section of forest land set aside by the Department of Fish and Game for development study

WHERE'S THE GOLD NEAR YOU?

If you're lucky enough to live in one of the gold areas listed below, then use Chapter 7 to find the best places to look for gold and start digging. If you don't live in a gold area, don't give up. The only reason the others are gold areas is because someone once found gold there. Someone had to be the first person to find the gold. You could be the lucky first person to find gold where you live. Good luck, prospector!

CANADA—Gold has been found in almost every province of Canada—British Columbia, Alberta,

Manitoba, Ontario, Quebec, Nova Scotia, the Yukon Territory and the Northwest Territories. Most of the Canadian gold areas were very rich, and the potential is great that prospectors will find even more gold now and in the future.

The best areas to search are the places where large deposits were found in the past. British Columbia's Fraser River, Cariboo Mountains and Williams Creek are good locations. In the Yukon Territory try panning the Yukon River, Klondike River, Quartz Creek and Bonanza Creek.

The recently developed Eskay Creek Gold Mine in British Columbia is said to have one of the best precious metal deposits in the world. The ore there contains gold, silver, copper and zinc.

There are many other good gold mining areas in Canada. In British Columbia look for gold in the Kootenay Valley, Kirkland Lake, Thompson Lake and the Rossland area. Porcupine Lake in the Yukon Territory and Lake Athabaska in Alberta both have gold. In the Northwest Territories search around Great Shave Lake, McKenzle Lake, Port Radium and the entire Yellowknife area. You can also hunt for silver on the north shore of Lake Superior and in Cobalt, Ontario.

For more information about where to find gold in Canada, contact the Mining Association of Canada, 1105-350 Sparks St., Ottawa, Ontario K1R 7S8, Canada.

ALABAMA—Gold was found here in the 1830s, and quite a bit of mining has been done. Gold has been found in Clay, Cleburne, Chilton, Coosa, Randolph, and Talladega counties. Contact the Geological Survey of Alabama, 420 Hackberry Lane, P.O. Drawer 0, University of Alabama, Tuscaloosa, Alabama 35486-4780.

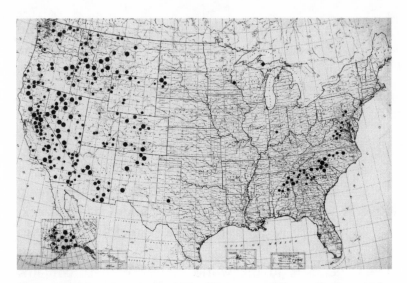

Map of gold locations in the U.S. (Courtesy of Keene Engineering)

ALASKA—The last gold frontier, this state still has areas that have been untouched by gold-seekers. There are over 60 different gold districts in Alaska. Contact the Alaska Division of Mines and Minerals, State Capital Building, Juneau, Alaska 99801, for information and directions to the various locations.

ARIZONA—People were placer mining here as early as 1774. The best areas have been the La Paz placer near the Colorado River and the Weaver-Rich Hill placers in southern Yavapai County. Good gold placers are found in all Arizona counties *except* Apache, Coconino, and Navajo. Contact the Arizona Department of Mines, 1502 W. Washington St., Phoenix, Arizona 85007-3210.

CALIFORNIA—More gold has come out of California than any other state. Gold is still found in the mountains, deserts, streams, dry washes, canyon walls and mountain tops. The "Mother Lode" area (where most of the gold

Gold-bearing areas in California. (Courtesy of California Division of Mines and Geology)

rush took place) runs about 200 miles through the foothills of the Sierra Nevada mountains, from Madera County in the south, up to Butte and Plumas counties in the north.

Most of the mountain ranges in southern California, as well as the high and low deserts, contain gold. A lot of gold has been found in the mountains of northern California, especially around the Trinity River. Smaller amounts of gold have been found in the Coast mountain ranges and the eastern side of the Sierra Nevada mountains.

The California Division of Mines and Geology puts out good booklets showing you exactly where to go. Write them at 801 K St. MS08-38, Sacramento, California 95814. There are so many prospecting and treasure hunting stores in the state, that there is bound to be one near you that can give you good tips on where to look.

COLORADO—Another big gold state. The most gold can be found around Denver and to the west and southwest. The best placer mining locations are in Boulder, Clear Creek, Costilla, Dolores, Eagle, Gilpin, Jefferson, Lake, Moffat, Park, Routt, San Juan, San Miguel, and Summit counties. Chaffee, Hinsdale, Mineral, and Montezuma counties are also good spots to look. For more information, write to the Colorado Mining Industrial Development Board, State Office Building, Denver, Colorado 80202.

For a real treat, visit the Colorado History Museum in Denver and see their mineral display. They have some gold nuggets that will make any prospector's heart skip a beat.

GEORGIA—Georgia was one of the first states to have a gold rush and is still one of the most popular areas for east coast prospectors.

All the gold deposits are located in the northern half of the state. The area around the town of Dahlonega, in Lumpkin County, has the most gold today. Other good areas are in Cherokee, Fulton, Hart, Madison, Rabun, Warren, and White counties. Write to the Georgia Department of Mines, Mining and Geology, 19 Hunter St. S.W., Atlanta, Georgia 30303.

IDAHO—Over 10 million ounces (284,000 kilograms) of gold have been mined in this state since the 1850s.

Boise County has the most gold, especially around the Boise Basin. The placer deposits of Idaho County also have gold, and over a million ounces (28,000 kilograms) have been found south of the town of Grangeville.

The Snake River has several areas with gold, as do Ada, Adams, Bingham, Bonneville, Camas, Caribou, Cassia, Clearwater, Custer, Elmore, Gem, Lemhi, Owyhee, Power, Shoshone, Twin Falls, Washington, and Valley counties. Write the Idaho Bureau of Mines and Geology, University of Idaho, Moscow, Idaho 83844.

MAINE—Most of Maine's gold has been found along the Swift River, and its feeder streams. Contact the Maine State Bureau of Mines, 184 State Street, Augusta, Maine 04333.

MASSACHUSETTS—You can find gold in western Massachusetts, around the towns of Bernardston, Blanford, and Charlemont and around Maxwell Brook. Contact the Office of the State Geologist, 100 Cambridge St., 20th Floor, Boston, Massachusetts 02202.

MICHIGAN—Gold has been found in northern Michigan around the town of Ishpeming. Contact the Michigan Department of Natural Resources, 1990 U.S. 41 South, Marquette, Michigan 49855.

MONTANA—This state has produced over 18 million ounces (510,000 kilograms) of gold for prospectors and miners since the first discovery. The richest area is in Alder Gulch, near Virginia City, in the southwest part of the state. Gold is found all along the western border of the state in Beaverhead, Lincoln, Mineral, Missoula,

Ravalli, and Sanders counties. Broadwater County has had more gold than any other part of the state.

Other gold areas are Deer Lodge, Fergus, Granite, Lewis and Clark, Park, Powell, and Silver Bow counties. For more information contact the Montana Bureau of Mines and Geology, Montana College of Mineral Science and Technology, Butte, Montana 59701.

NEVADA—Gold is found in every county in Nevada *except* for Lincoln. The biggest gold placer deposits are in Charleston, Mountain City, and Tuscarora districts in Elko County. Also look in the Lynn District in Eureka County, the Battle Mountain District in Lander County, the Gold Canyon District in Lyon County, the Rawhide District in Mineral County, the Manhattan and Round Mountain districts in Nye County, the Sawtooth and Spring Valley districts in Pershing County, and the Osceola District in White Pine County.

A letter to the Nevada Bureau of Mines, University of Nevada, Reno, Nevada 89507 will get you plenty of information.

Special Note: Nevada is the "silver state," so keep your eyes open for that "blue muck" when you're out. Any blue clay material may contain both gold and silver.

NEW MEXICO—A "gold belt" runs through the middle of this state, from the southwest part to the north-central part. Two and a half million dollars of gold have been found here. Grant County has had the most gold, but gold has also been found in Colfax, Hildalgo, Lincoln, Otero, Rio Arriba, Sandoval, Santa Fe, and Taos counties. Sierra County has had the second largest amount of gold in the state, and recently has been the best place to find gold.

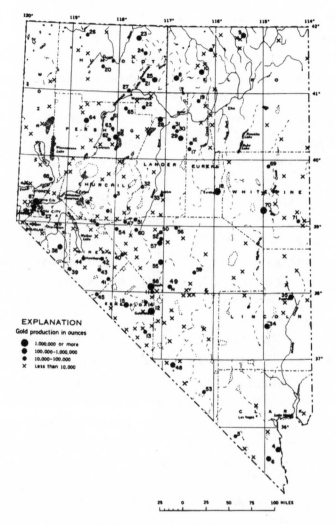

Sites where gold has been found in Nevada. (Courtesy of Nevada Bureau of Mines)

Small amounts of gold have been found in Bernalillo, Dona Ana, Mora, and San Miguel counties. Contact the New Mexico State Bureau of Mines, New Mexico Institute of Mining, Socorro, New Mexico 87801, or check with prospecting supply stores in these areas.

NEW YORK—Gold has been found in the Adirondack Mountains, on the Upper Hudson River, on the Black River, and in Lewis and Jefferson counties. You can also try your luck looking for silver in St. Lawrence County. People are finding silver there right now.

For more information, contact the New York State Geological Survey, 3136 Cultural Education Center, Albany, New York 12230.

NORTH CAROLINA—North Carolina is a very popular area for east coast prospectors today. Nearly 2 million ounces (57,000 kilograms) of gold have been found, including several large nuggets. One nugget that weighed 272 ounces (8 kilograms) was found by a young boy in Cabarrus County.

The Gold Hill District in Rowan County has the most gold. Placer gold deposits have also been found in Burke, Cabarrus, Catawba, Davidson, Franklin, Gaston, Guilford, Lincoln, Mecklenburg, Montgomery, Moore, Nash, Randolph, Transylvania, Union, Warren, Yadkin and several other counties. Contact The North Carolina Division of Mineral Resources, State Office Building, Raleigh, North Carolina 27600.

OREGON—A very productive state, with several gold rushes and 6 million ounces (170,000 kilograms) of gold found, Oregon is a popular area for prospectors today. Silver was also discovered in the Rogue River Valley and the Bohemia district of Douglas County.

The best gold areas are the southwestern corner of the state and the eastern border with Idaho. Baker County has had the most gold—over a million and a half ounces (43,000 kilograms). Gold is also found in Coos, Crook, Curry, Douglas, Grant, Jackson,

Josephine, Malheur, Union, and Wheeler counties. Contact the Oregon State Department of Geology and Mineral Industries, 1069 State Office Building, Portland, Oregon 97201.

SOUTH CAROLINA—The northwestern part of the state and the area along the Georgia border have the most gold. The best area today for prospectors is in Chesterfield County, where some people claim you can get an ounce or two a day with a little know-how and a lot of luck.

The other gold areas are in Cherokee, Chester, Greenville, Kershaw, Lancaster, McCormick, Spartenberg, Union, and York counties. The South Carolina Division of Geology, State Development Board, P.O. Box 927, Columbus, South Carolina 29200 is a very good source of information.

SOUTH DAKOTA—This state is the third biggest gold producer, with 35 million ounces (992,000 kilograms) found! Most gold has come from the rich Homestake Mine in Lawrence County. Placer gold is also found in Custer and Pennington counties. There aren't as many prospectors in this state, so it may be easier to get lucky. Contact the South Dakota State Geological Survey, Science Center, University of South Dakota, Vermillion, South Dakota 57069.

TEXAS—Placer gold is said to be found in the Panhandle region of Texas and in the central portion of the state. For more information, contact the Texas Bureau of Economic Geology, University of Texas, Austin, Texas 78712.

UTAH—Nearly 20 million ounces (567,000 kilograms) of gold has been found in Utah. The Bingham District has had the most gold, but Beaver, Daggett, Emery, Garfield, Grand, Juab, Kane, Millard, Piute, Salt Lake, San Juan, Sevier, Tooele, Uintah and Utah counties also have gold. Contact the Utah Geological and Mineral Survey, University of Utah, Salt Lake City, Utah 84102.

VERMONT—Quite a bit of gold has been found in Vermont over the years. There was even a minor rush here in the late 1800s. One of the most popular areas for today's prospector is around Plymouth Five Corners. The Rock, Mad, White, West, Williams, Ottauquechee, Little, Lamoille, Gihon, and Missisquoi rivers all have gold in certain areas. The Vermont Division of Geology and Earth Resources, 103 S. Main St., Center Building, Waterbury, Vermont 05671 can give you more information.

VIRGINIA—Gold was first reported here in the 1780s, and nearly 200,000 ounces (6000 kilograms) have been found since then. The gold belt runs through the central part of the state and gold is found in Albemarle, Buckingham, Culpeper, Cumberland, Fauquier, Fluvanna, Goochland, Louisa, Orange, Prince William, Spotsylvania, and Stafford counties. Contact the Virginia Department of Conservation and Economic Development, Division of Mineral Resources, Natural Resources Building, Box 3667, Charlottesville, Virginia 22901.

WASHINGTON—Gold is found in many areas of Washington, but mostly in the northern part of the state. About three and a half million ounces (99,000 kilograms) have been found. Recreational prospectors do very well here today because there aren't as many miners as in other "gold states." The counties where gold is found include:

Chelan, Clallam, Ferry, Garfield, Grays Harbor, Kittitas, Lincoln, Okanogan, Pacific, Snohomish, Stevens and Whatcom. Write to the Washington Division of Mines and Geology, Department of Conservation, 335 General Administration Building, Olympia, Washington 82501.

WYOMING—Gold is spread all over this state, with Fremont County having the most. Gold is also found in Albany, Crook, Johnson, Lincoln, Park, Sheridan, Sublette, Sweetwater, and Teton counties. Write to the Geological Survey of Wyoming, University of Wyoming, Laramie, Wyoming 82070 for details on various areas.

The following states aren't "gold states," but some gold has been found. Try contacting a local outdoor supply store or the Geology Department of a local university for information on exactly where to search for gold in these states.

CONNECTICUT—Take your pan and shovel to Beacon Falls, Beacon Hill Brook, and Lead Mine Brook to find gold. You may also have some luck around the town of Harwinton.

INDIANA—A small amount of gold has been found in south central Indiana.

MARYLAND—Gold has been found in the area around Great Falls.

MISSOURI—There has been some gold found in several of the rivers here.

NEW HAMPSHIRE—There are reports of gold in some

of the stream beds in northeastern New Hampshire, along the Maine border.

OKLAHOMA—The southern parts of the state have placer gold deposits. There have even been a few small rushes here.

PENNSYLVANIA—There have been reports of small amounts of gold found in the streams of this state.

RHODE ISLAND—There are several reports of gold found in this state near the towns of Glocester and Foster.

Other states, such as **ARKANSAS** and **ILLINOIS**, have produced small amounts of gold in the past, but not enough is known about the finds to give any accurate details.

C H A P T E R

10

HOW TO TALK
LIKE A MINER!

The miners and prospectors of the old days left their mark on us. We all say things that relate to mining, prospecting, and the gold rush. Use these phrases and you too can talk like a miner.

All that glitters is not gold—This phrase comes from an old proverb dating back to ancient Roman times. During the gold rush it referred to fool's gold, which is bright and glittery in the pan, but is worth nothing. Today it means that even if something looks good, it's possible that it's not.

El Dorado—During their conquest of South America, the Spanish heard of a place with so much gold that the people there coated their king with it once a year and called him "El Dorado," meaning "The Painted One." During the gold rush, miners would

say that they found "El Dorado" when they found a place with lots of gold. Today "El Dorado" means something very hard, or even impossible, to find.

Eureka—Comes from a Greek word meaning "I have found it." Supposedly, Archimedes, a famous Greek inventor, said this when he discovered a way to tell the purity of a gold object. When a miner found a rich area of gold he would shout, "Eureka!"

Hit pay dirt—The gold in placer deposits is mostly found in one area of dirt, while the areas around it have no gold. A miner digs until he finds the layer with gold—this is the "pay dirt." Today it means to work hard and finally get what you want.

Hit rock bottom—When a miner digs out all the pay dirt until he hits bedrock and runs out of gold, he has "hit rock bottom." Today it means when things are as bad as they can get.

It's a gold mine—When someone has an idea or business that will surely make them a lot of money, we say "it's a gold mine."

It didn't pan out—If a prospector pans some dirt to see if there is any gold and finds none, then "things didn't pan out." Today it means things didn't work out the way we wanted them to.

Strike it rich—When a miner hits a rock wall or a gravel deposit with his shovel and sees gold, he has "struck it rich." Today it means to get lucky.

GOLD FEVER QUIZ

ANSWER *TRUE* OR *FALSE*

1 John Sutter found the first piece of gold that started the gold rush.

2 Only 10% of the gold still remains to be found in California.

3 All you really need to prospect for gold is a gold pan and a shovel.

4 James Marshall got rich in the gold rush.

5 Only people born in California were allowed to mine in the gold rush.

6 You can look for gold on private property.

7 The first piece of gold found in California was discovered under a tree.

8 A sluice box is used to prospect where there is no water.

9 The roots of trees on stream banks are good places to look for gold.

10 No kids have found any gold yet.

Turn the page upside down for the answers.

ANSWERS

1. False. James Marshall found the first piece of gold.

2. False. 90% of California's gold remains to be found.

3. True. The other equipment will just make it easier.

4. False. James Marshall died a poor man.

5. False. People came from all over the world to seek their fortune.

6. True. But get the owner's permission first.

7. True. The first piece of California gold was found under a tree called "The Oak of the Golden Dream." The gold was attached to the root of an onion

8. False. A dry washer is used when there's no water.

9. True. Gold gets stuck in the roots of trees along stream banks, so these are good places to check.

10. False. Lots and lots of kids have struck it rich. And you could be next!

Turn to the next page to see if you have gold fever!

SCORING

1–3 correct: You'd better read the book one more time or you may never strike it rich.

4–6 correct: You're getting better, but you still need to watch out for that "fool's gold."

7–8 correct: You're on your way to pay dirt.

9–10 correct: Eureka! You're a real prospector. The lost "Cavern of Gold" should be an easy find for you!

END NOTES

1. Charles B. Gilespie, "Marshall's Own Account of the Gold Discovery," *Century Magazine* (February 1891): 520.

2. Charles B. Gilespie, "Marshall's Own Account of the Gold Discovery," *Century Magazine* (February 1891): 520.

3. *The California Gold Rush* (New York: American Heritage Publishing, 1961), 18.

4. Charles B. Gilespie, "Marshall's Own Account of the Gold Discovery," *Century Magazine* (February 1891): 520.

5. Charles B. Gilespie, "Marshall's Own Account of the Gold Discovery," *Century Magazine* (February 1891): 520.

6. *The California Gold Rush* (New York: American Heritage Publishing, 1961), 19.

7. Louise Clappe, *The Shirley Letters from the California Mines 1851–1852* (New York: Ballentine Books, 1949), 20.

ABOUT THE AUTHOR

JAMES KLEIN is an actor, author, recognized gold expert, and real-life prospector! He has appeared as a gold-prospecting expert on ABC, CBS, and NBC television, on various radio programs, and has been featured in articles in *The LA Times* and several other newspapers. He is a frequent guest on television talk shows, and has had roles in such movies as *Tom Horn*, *Coming Home*, *The China Syndrome*, *The Electric Horseman*, and *City of Angels*.

James has written six other bestselling books about gold for adults. He currently spends much of his time leading school programs and outdoor groups, and speaking to children about his favorite topics—gold and prospecting!